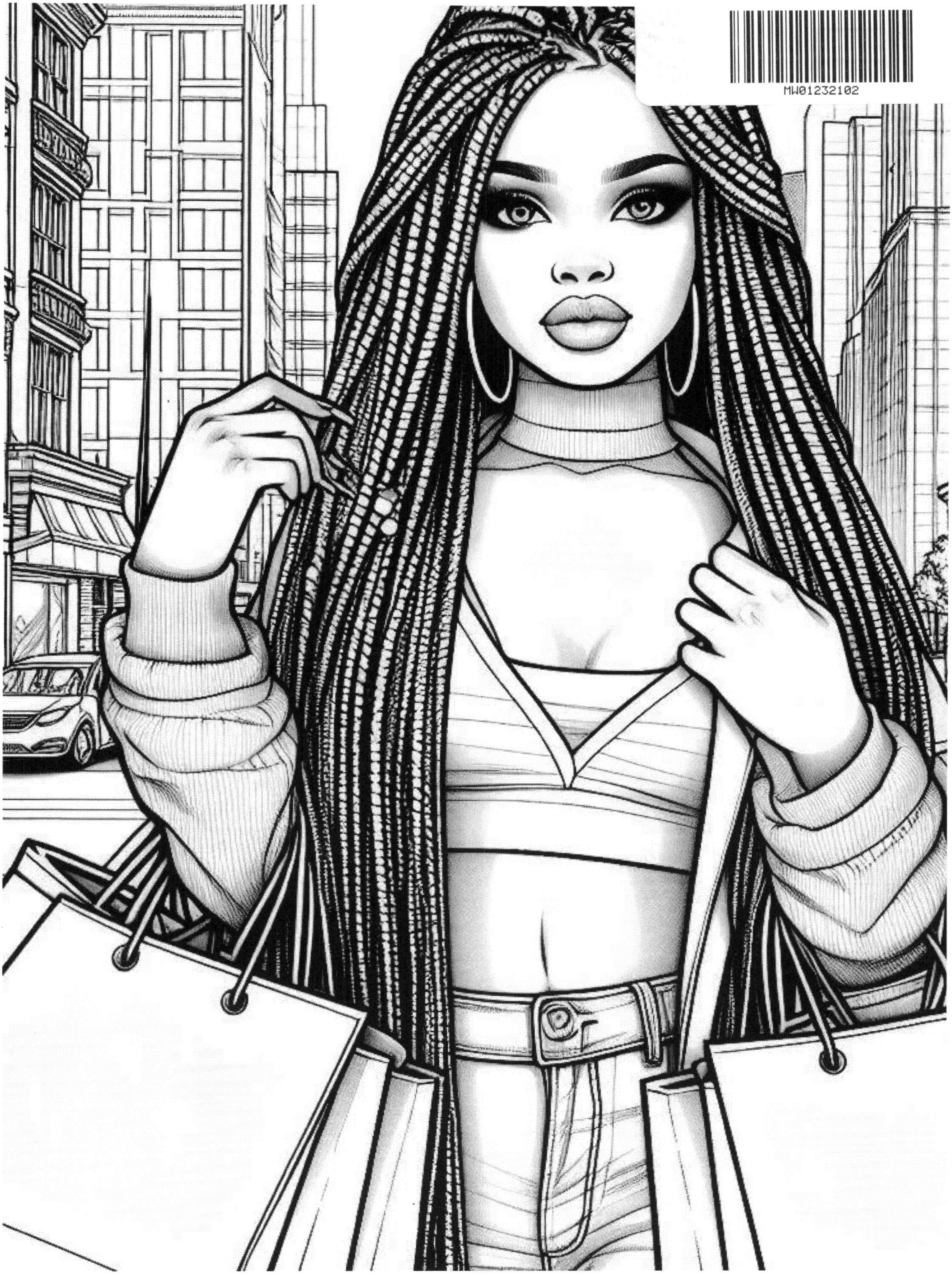

MW01232102

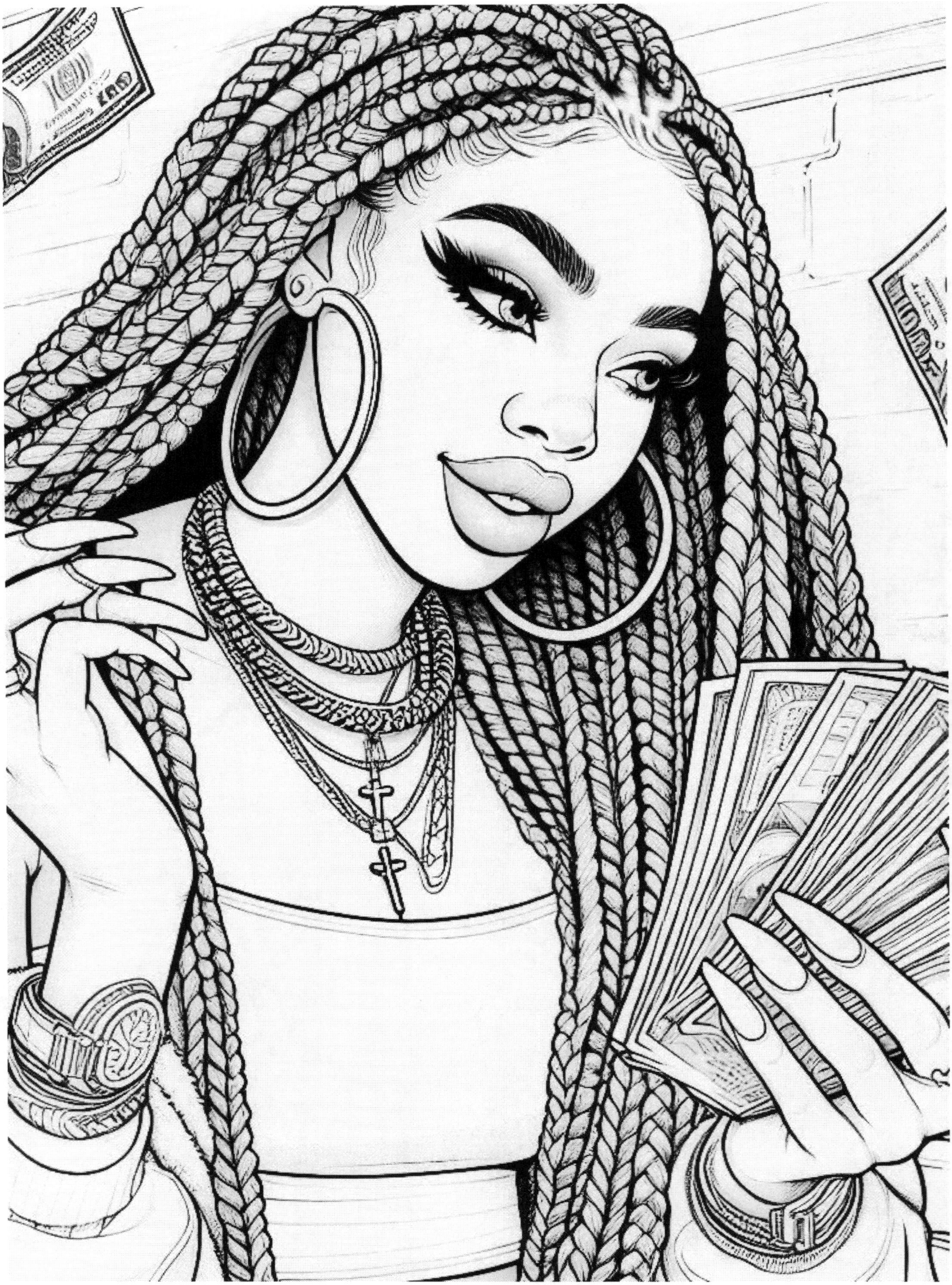

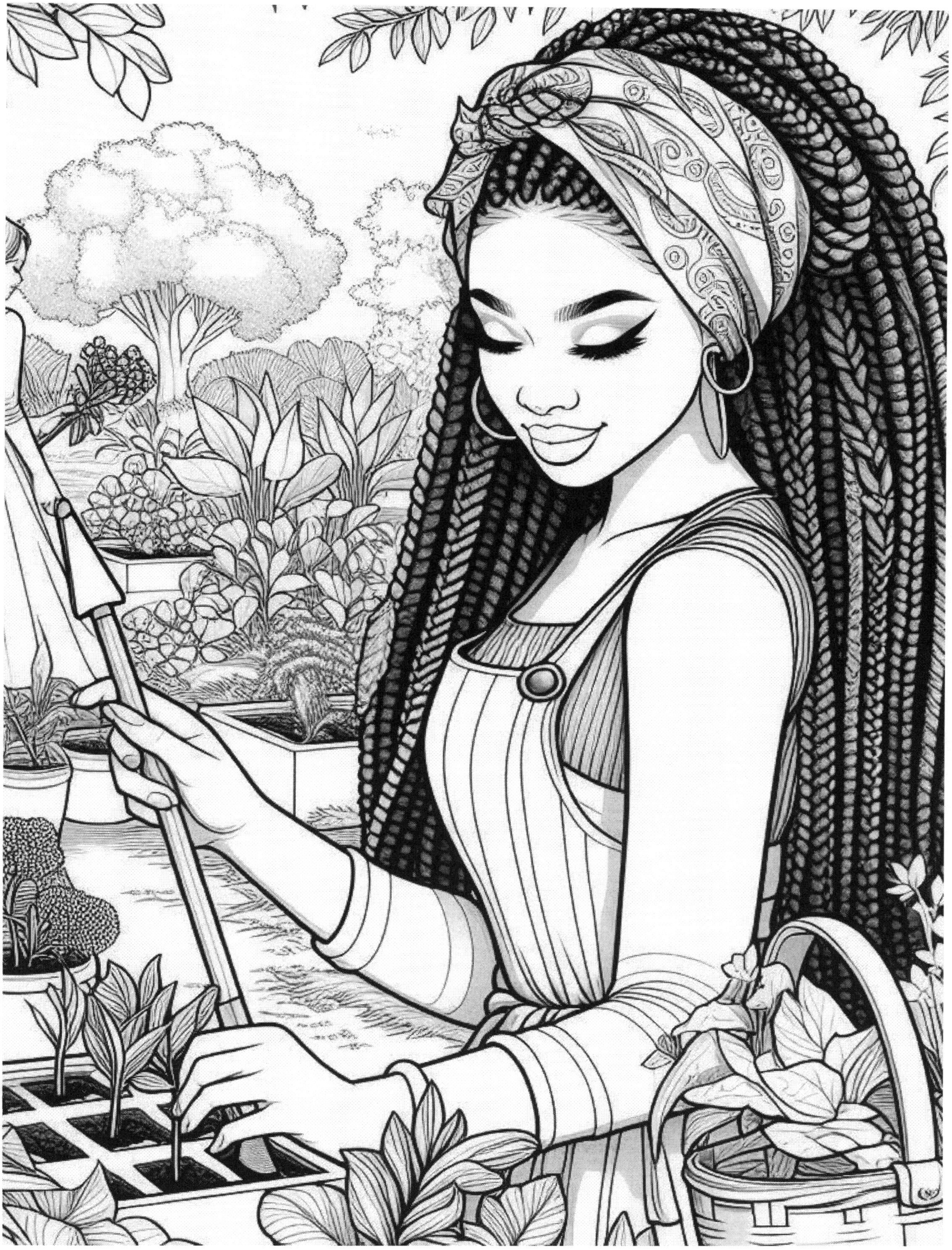

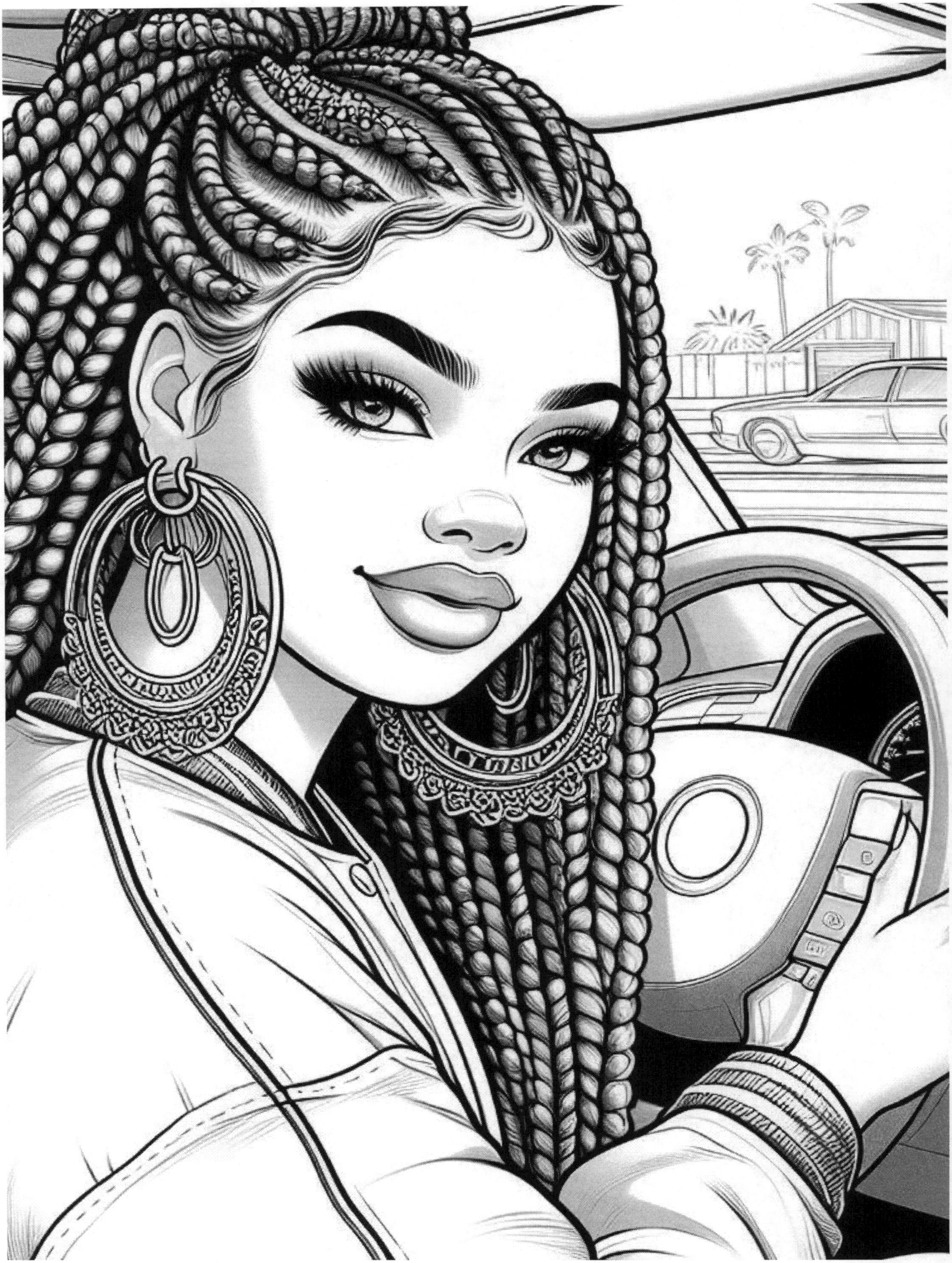

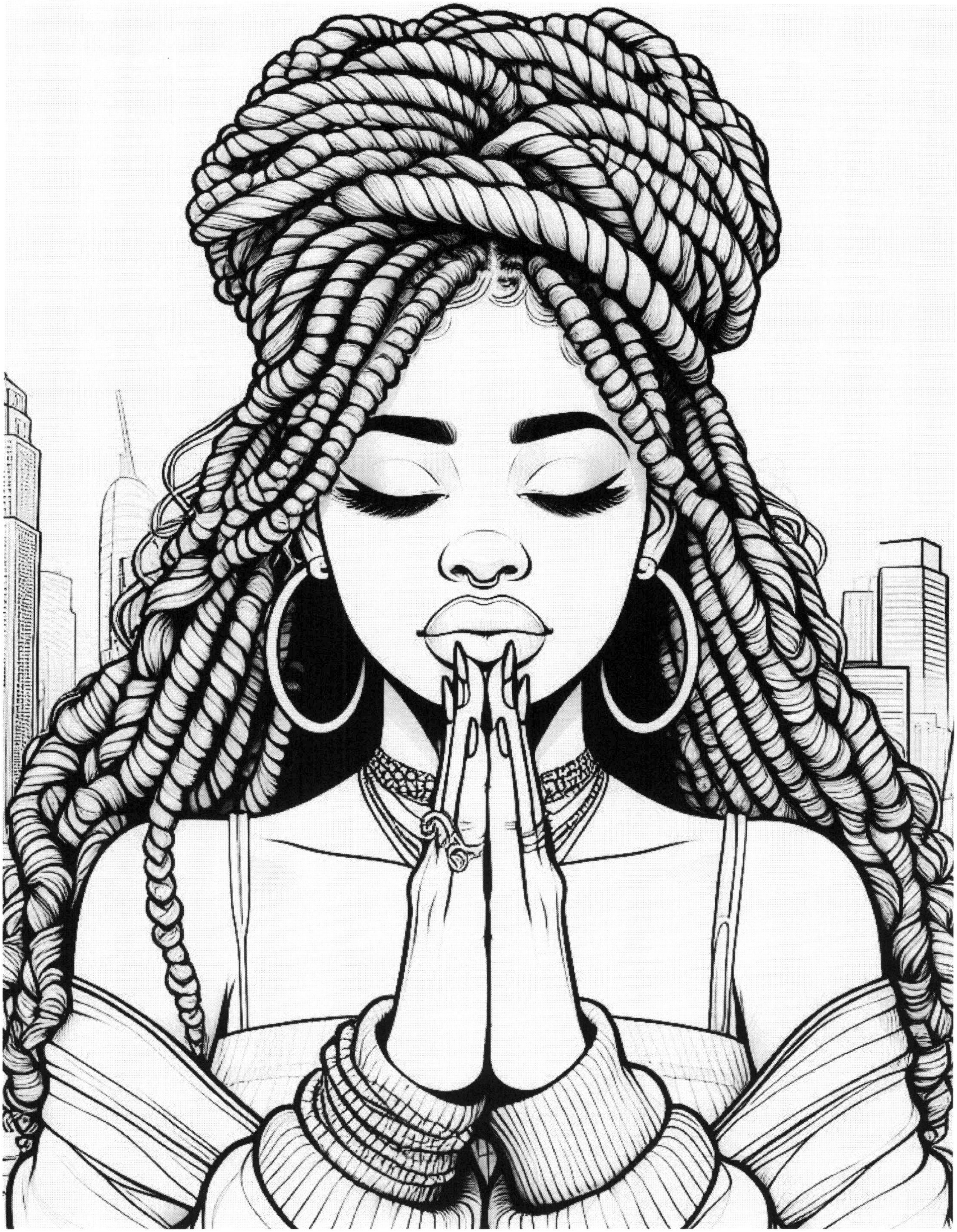

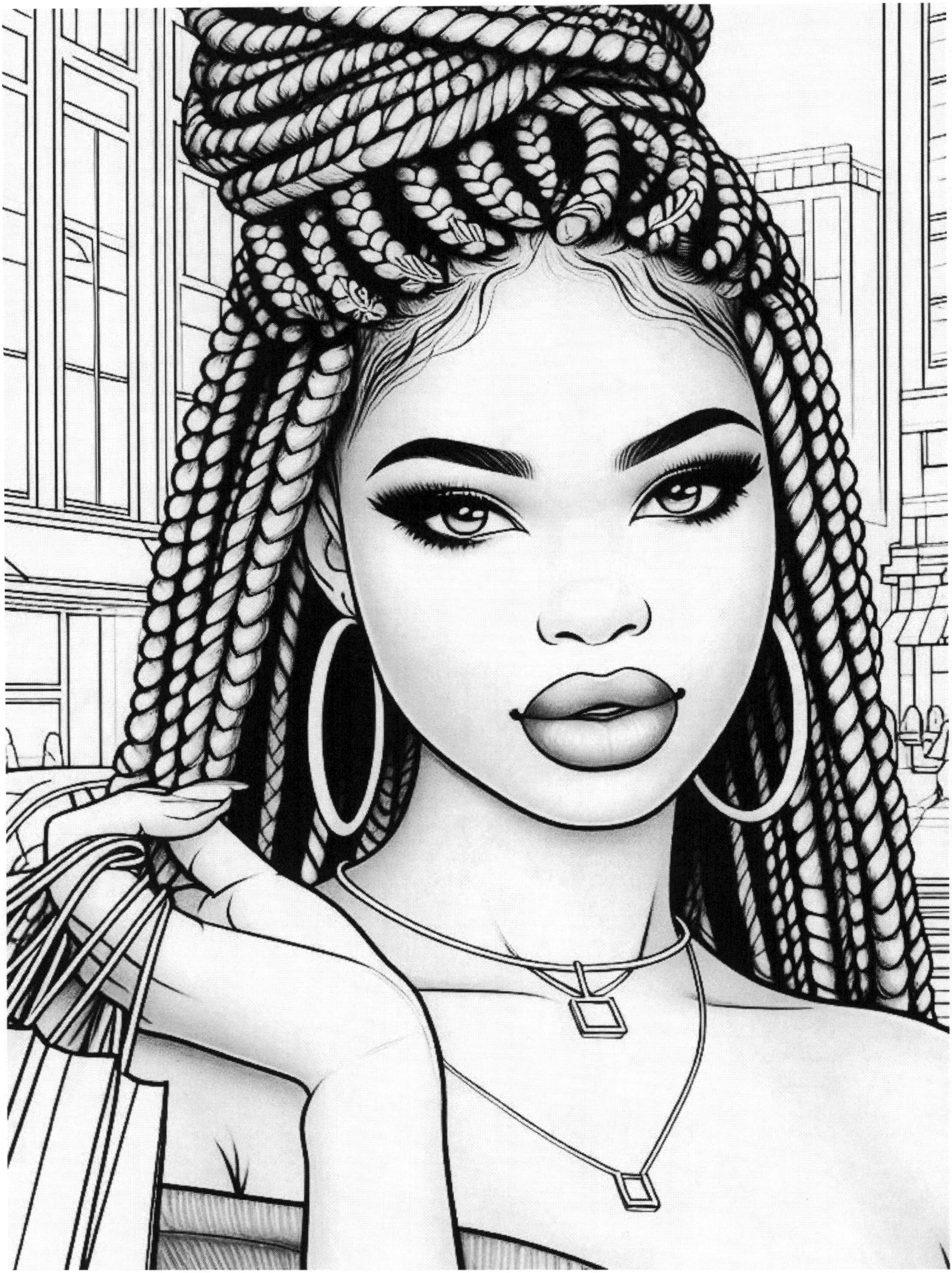

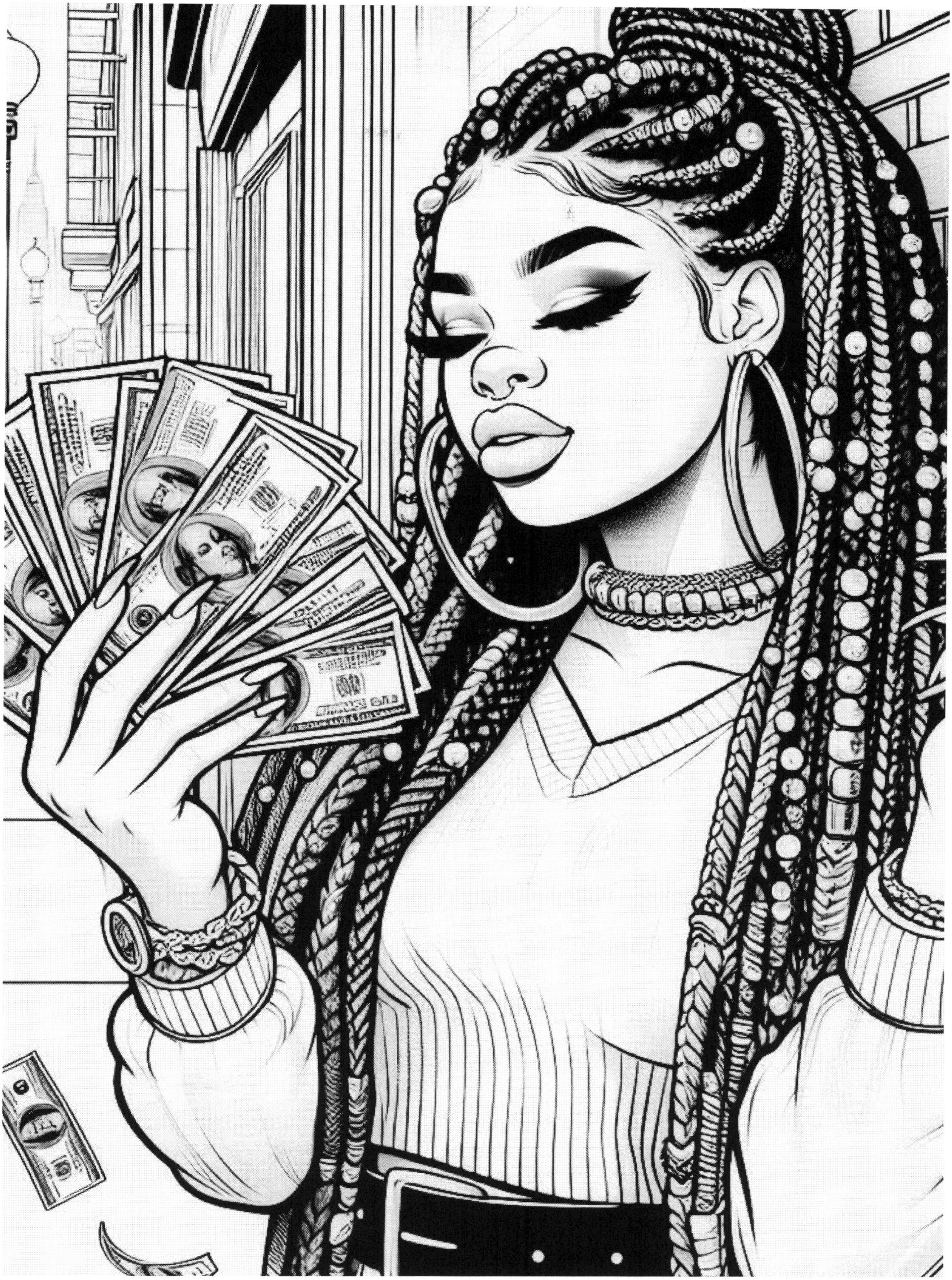

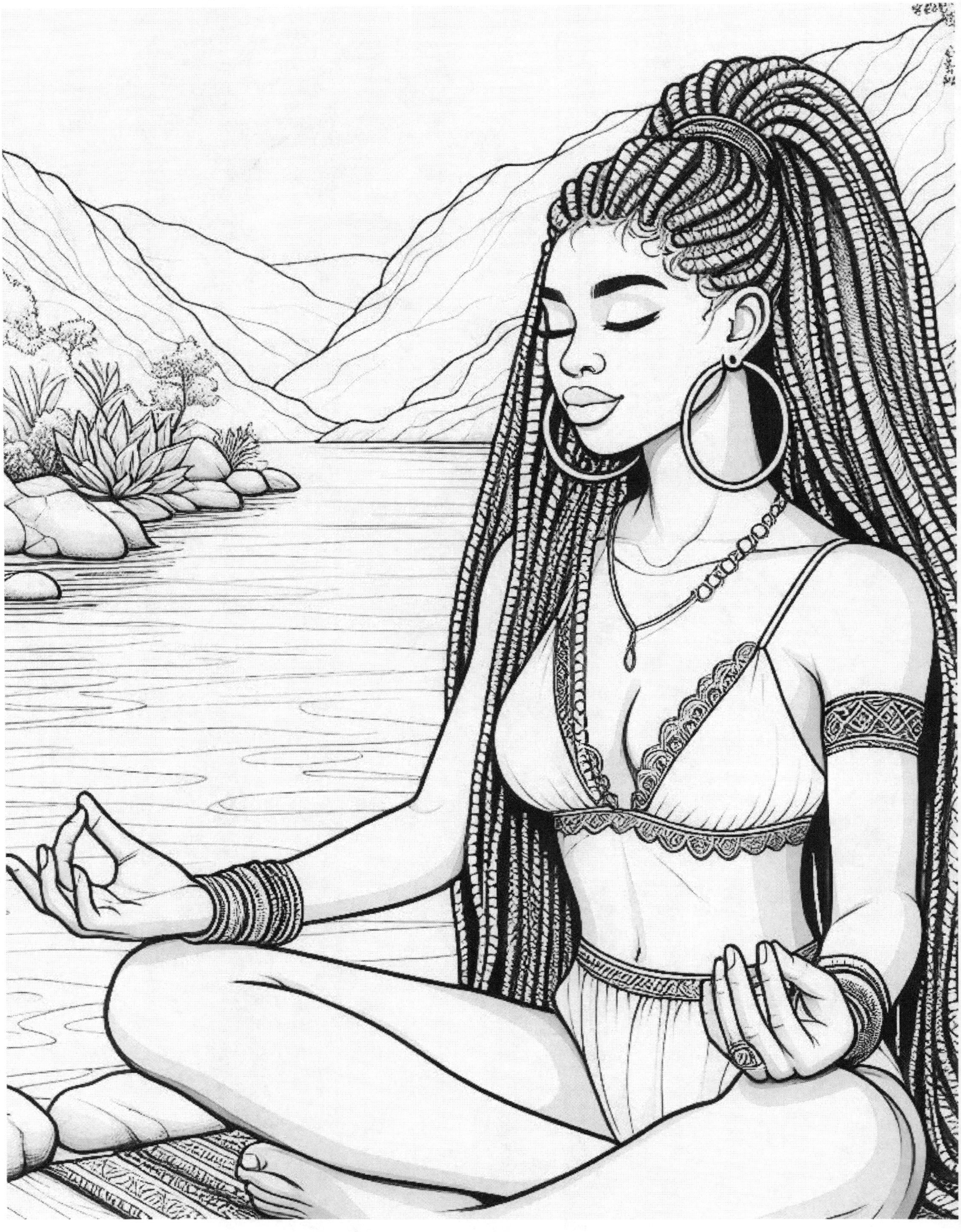

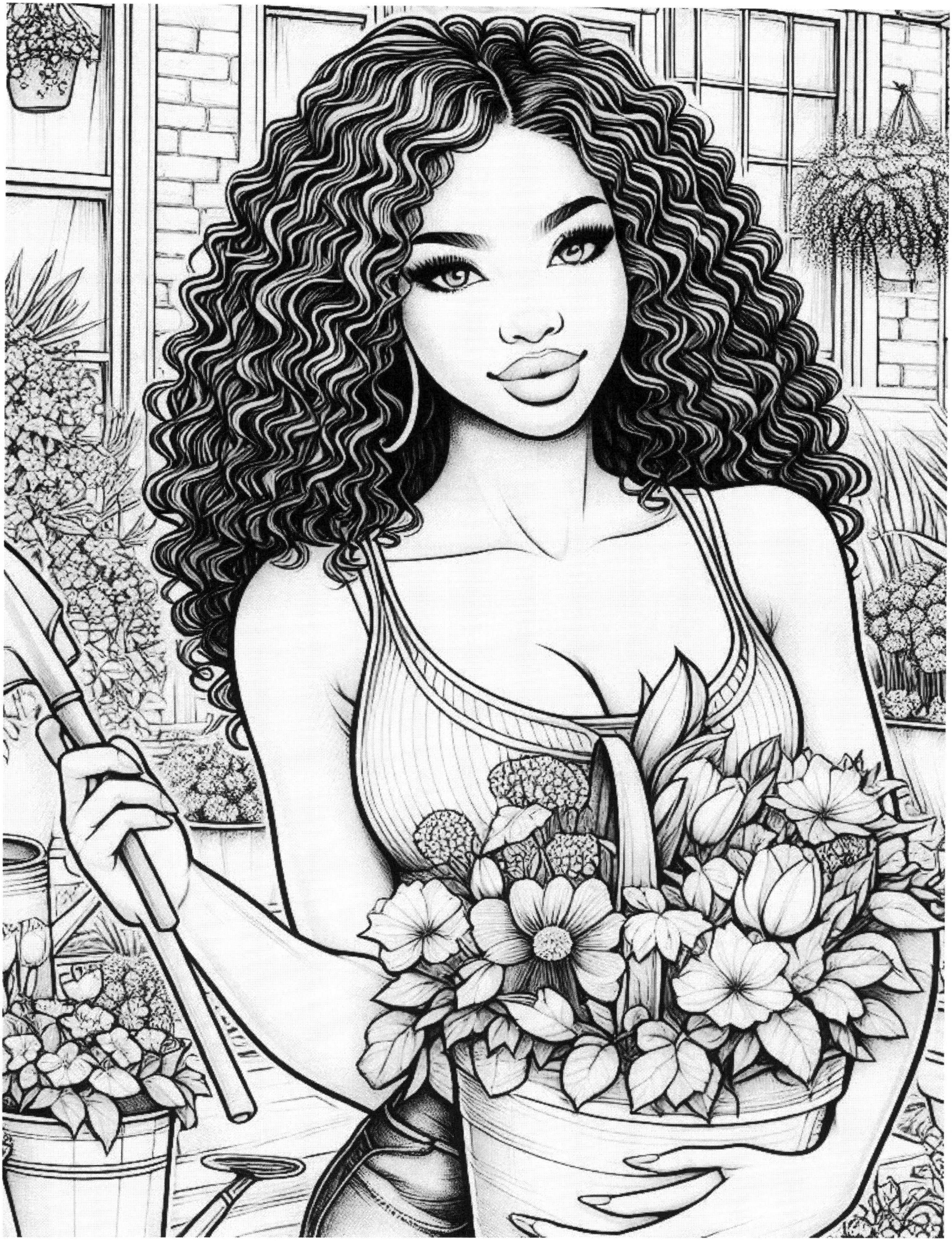

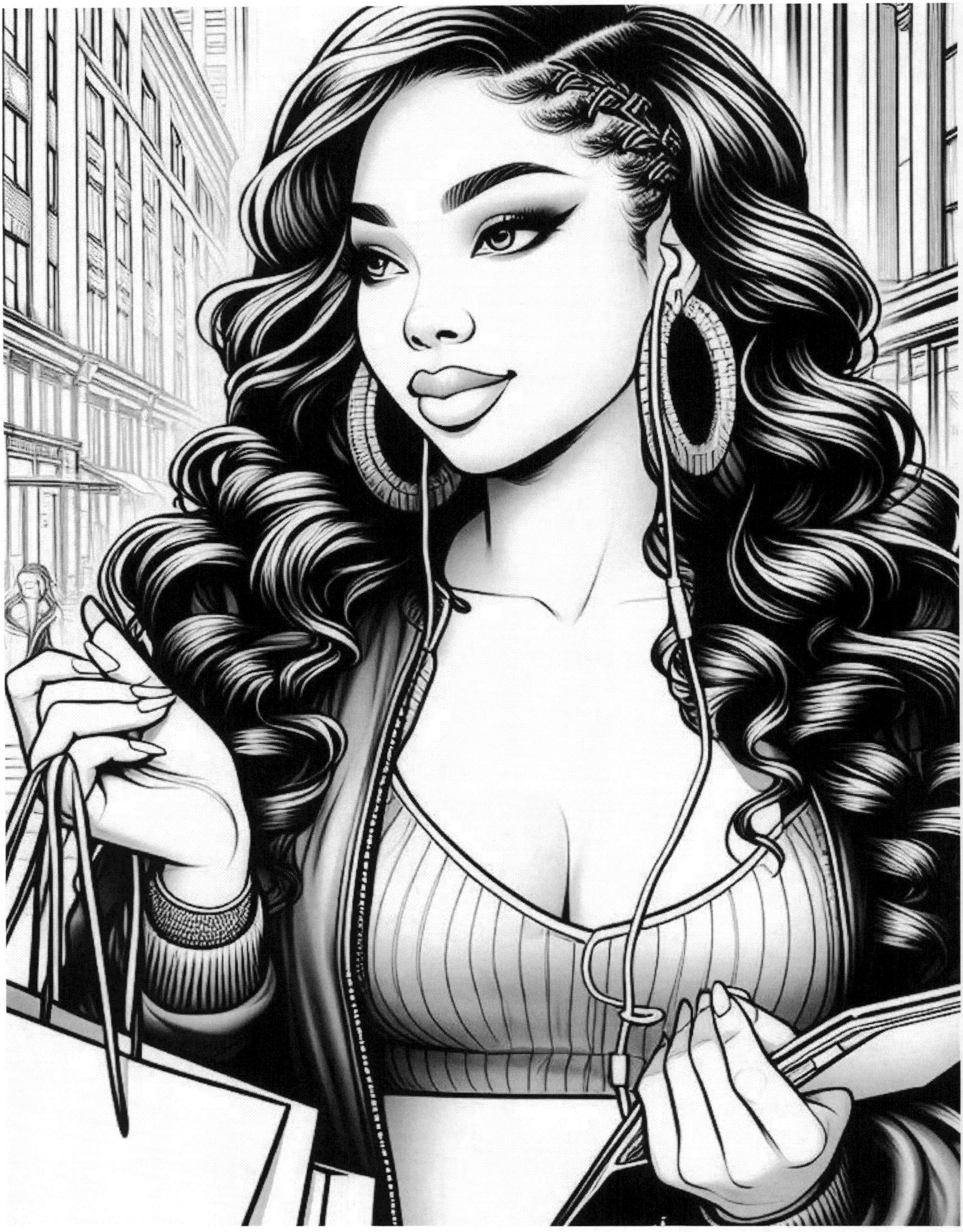

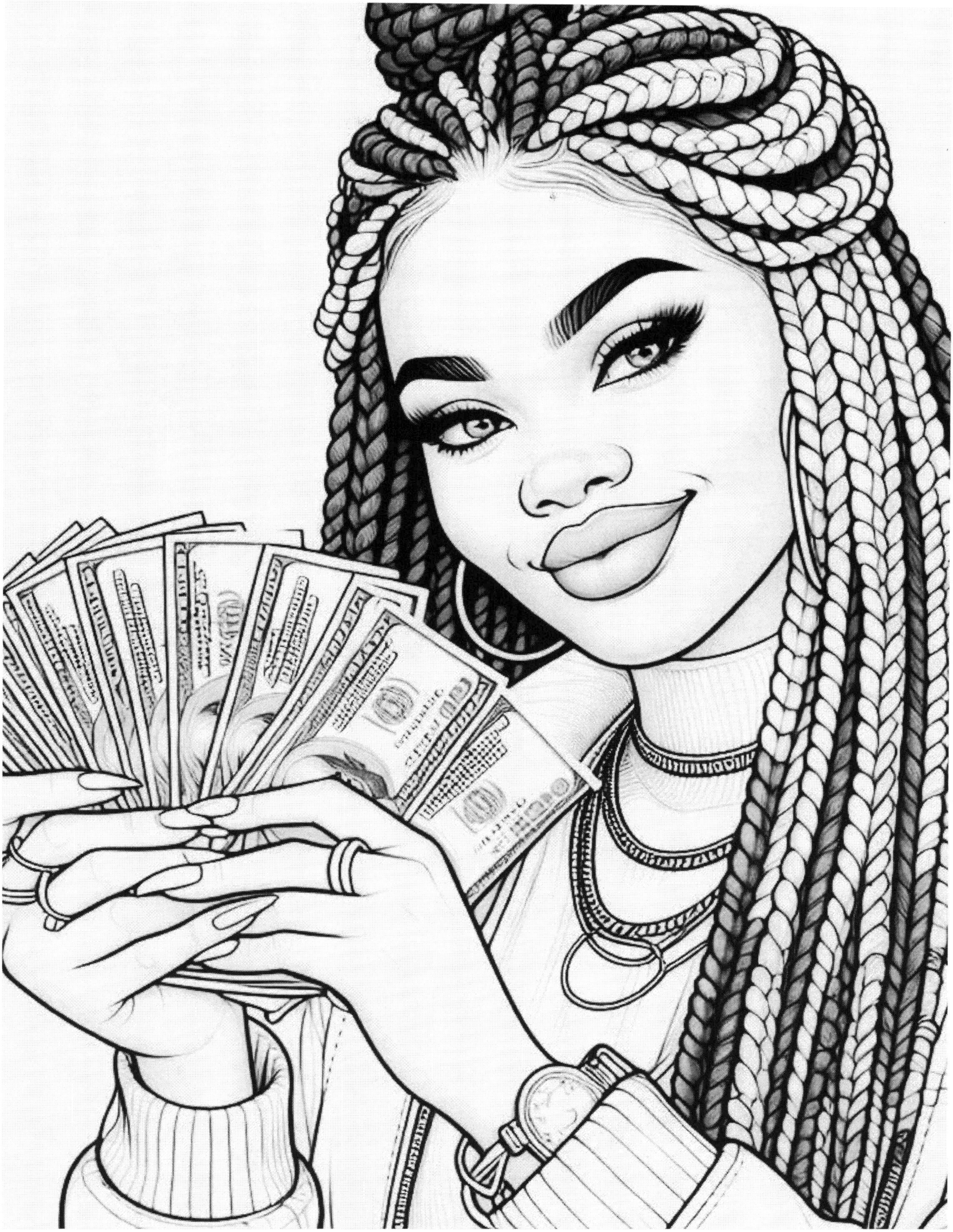

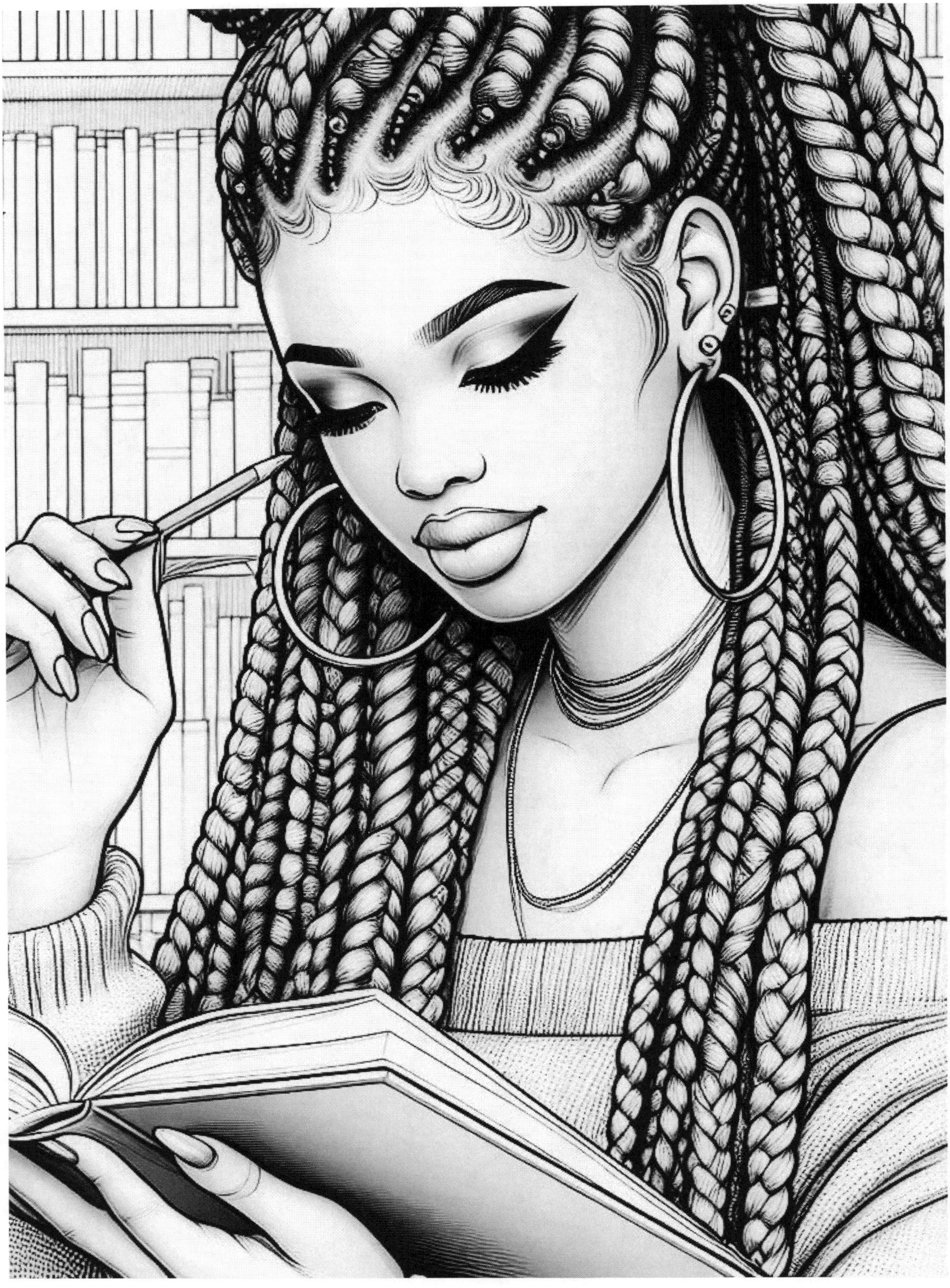

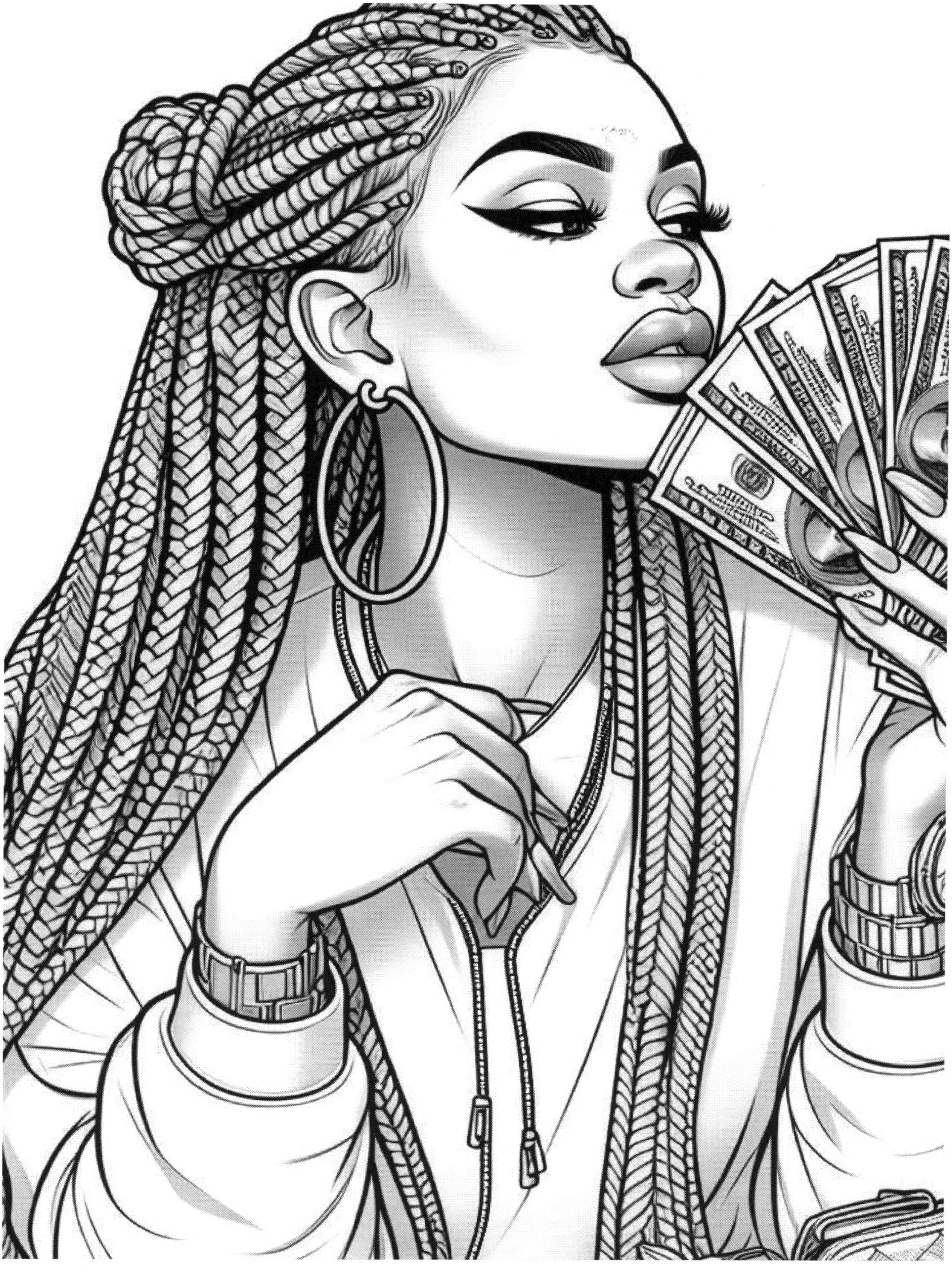

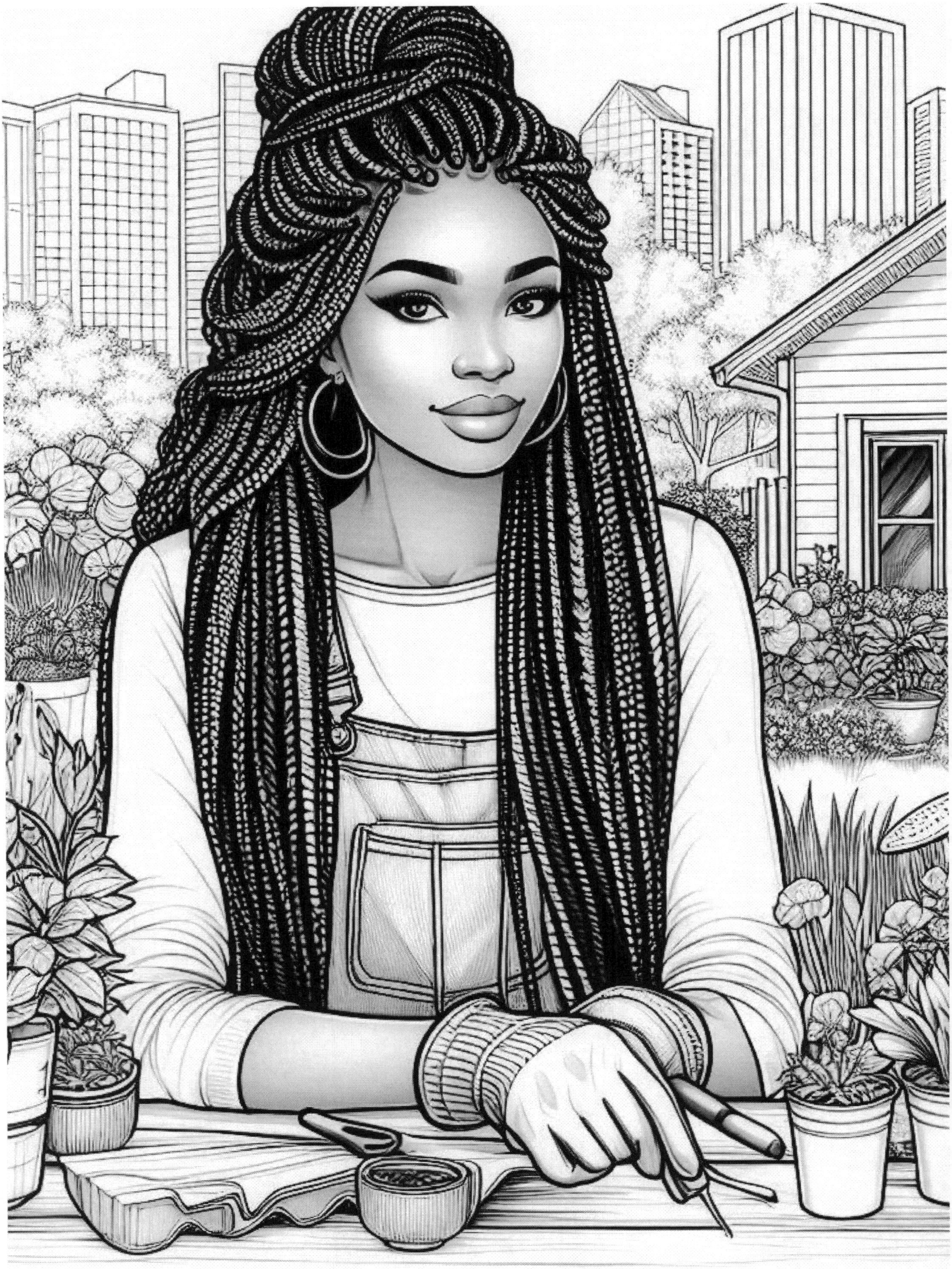

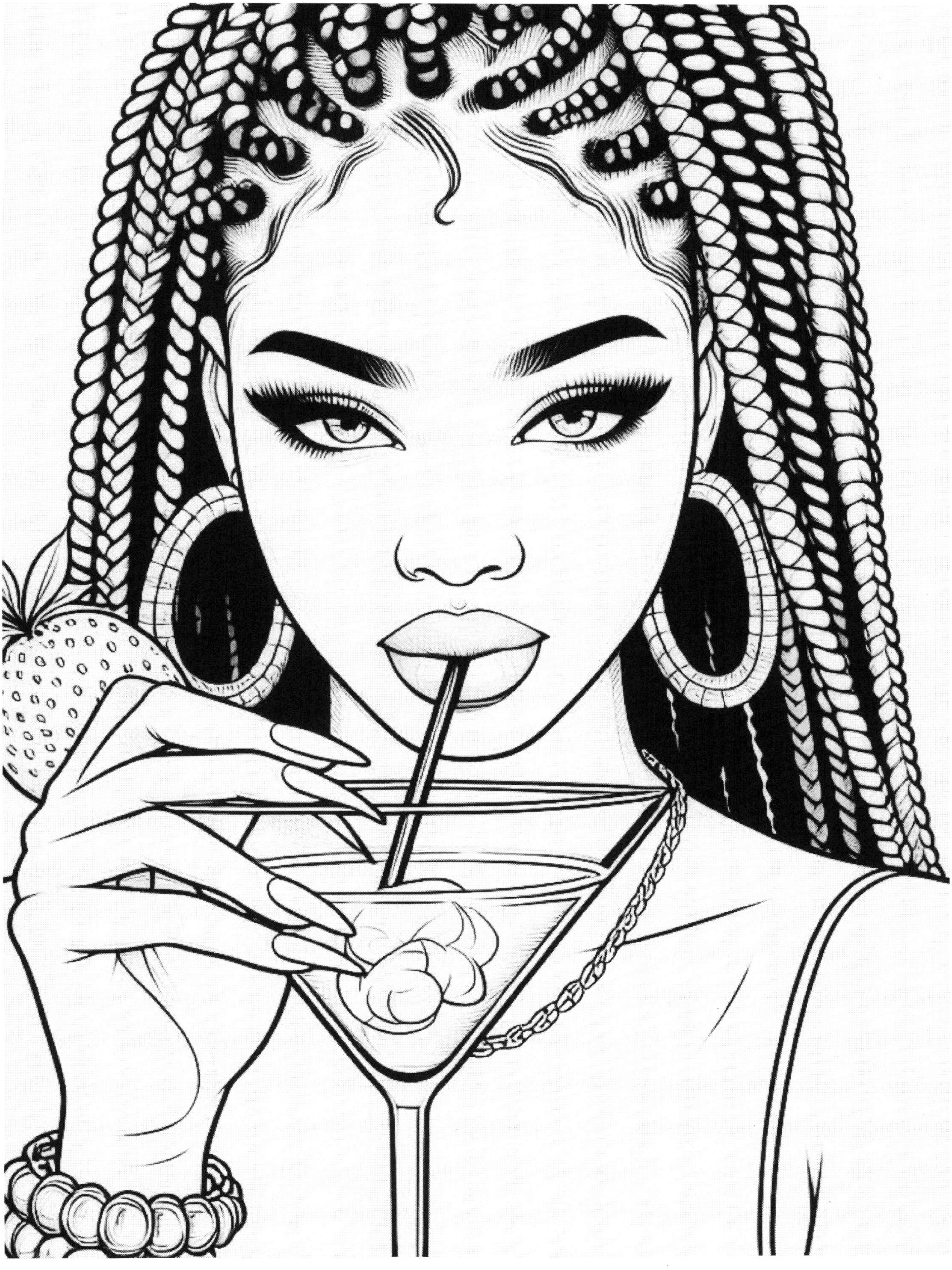

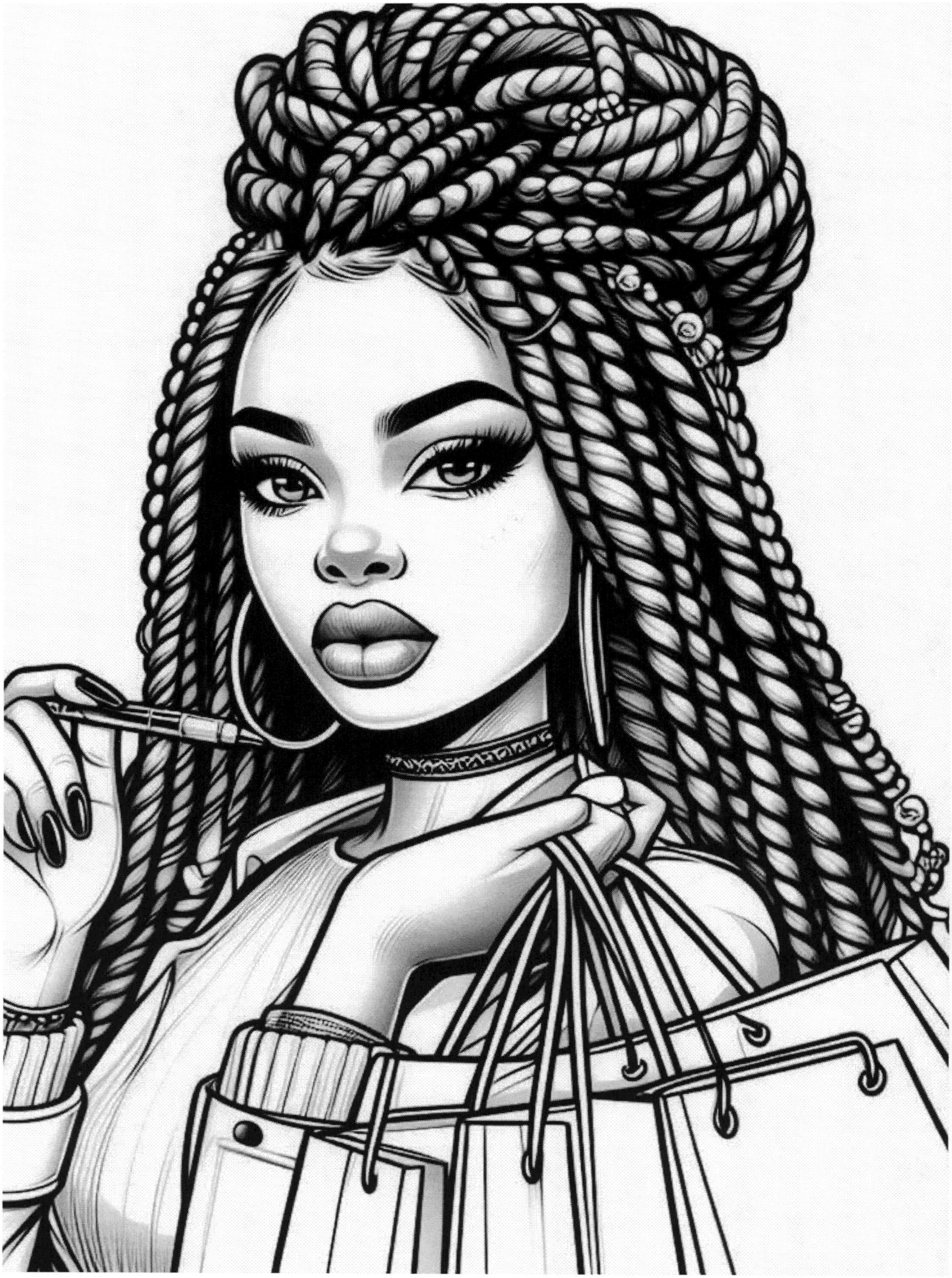

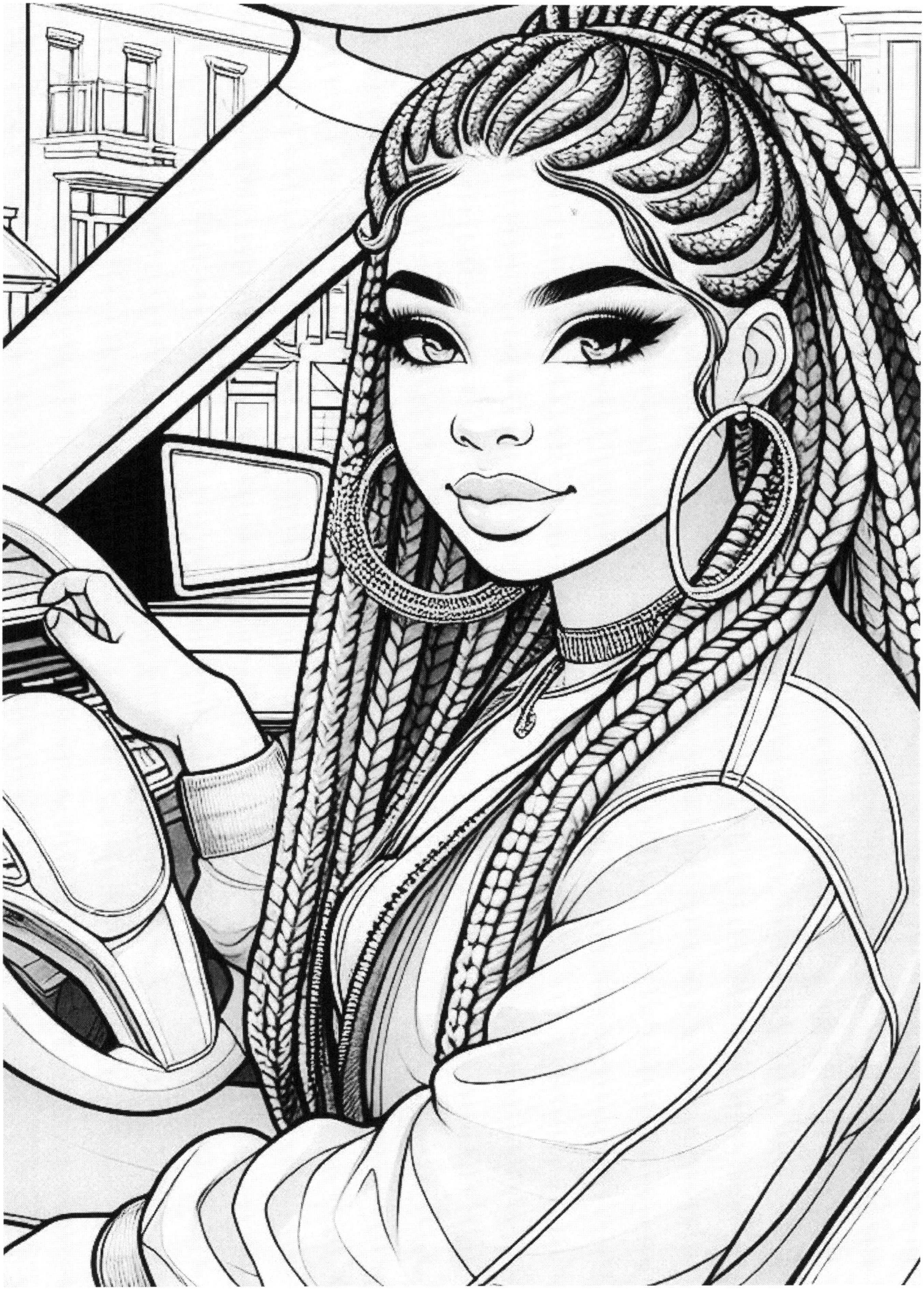

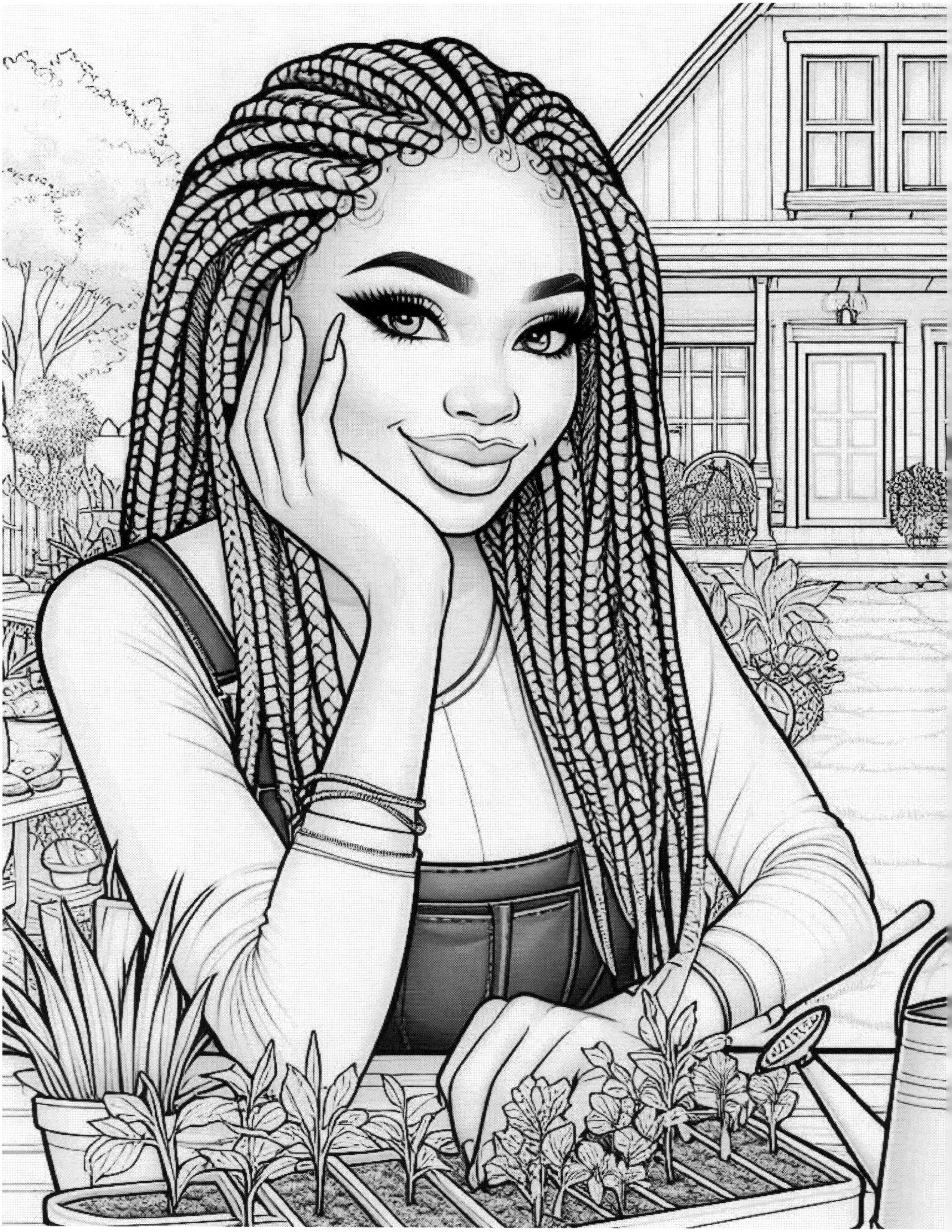

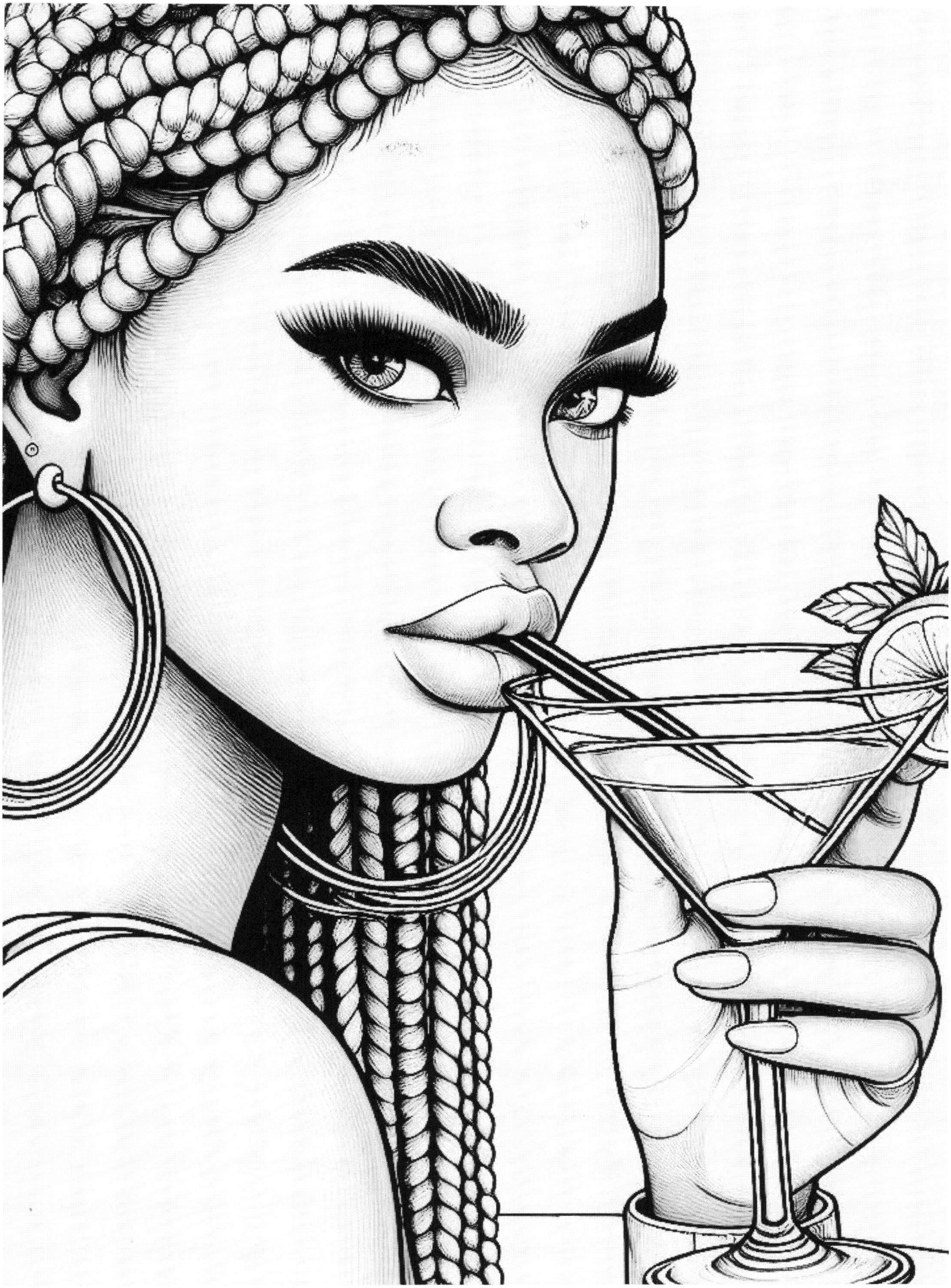

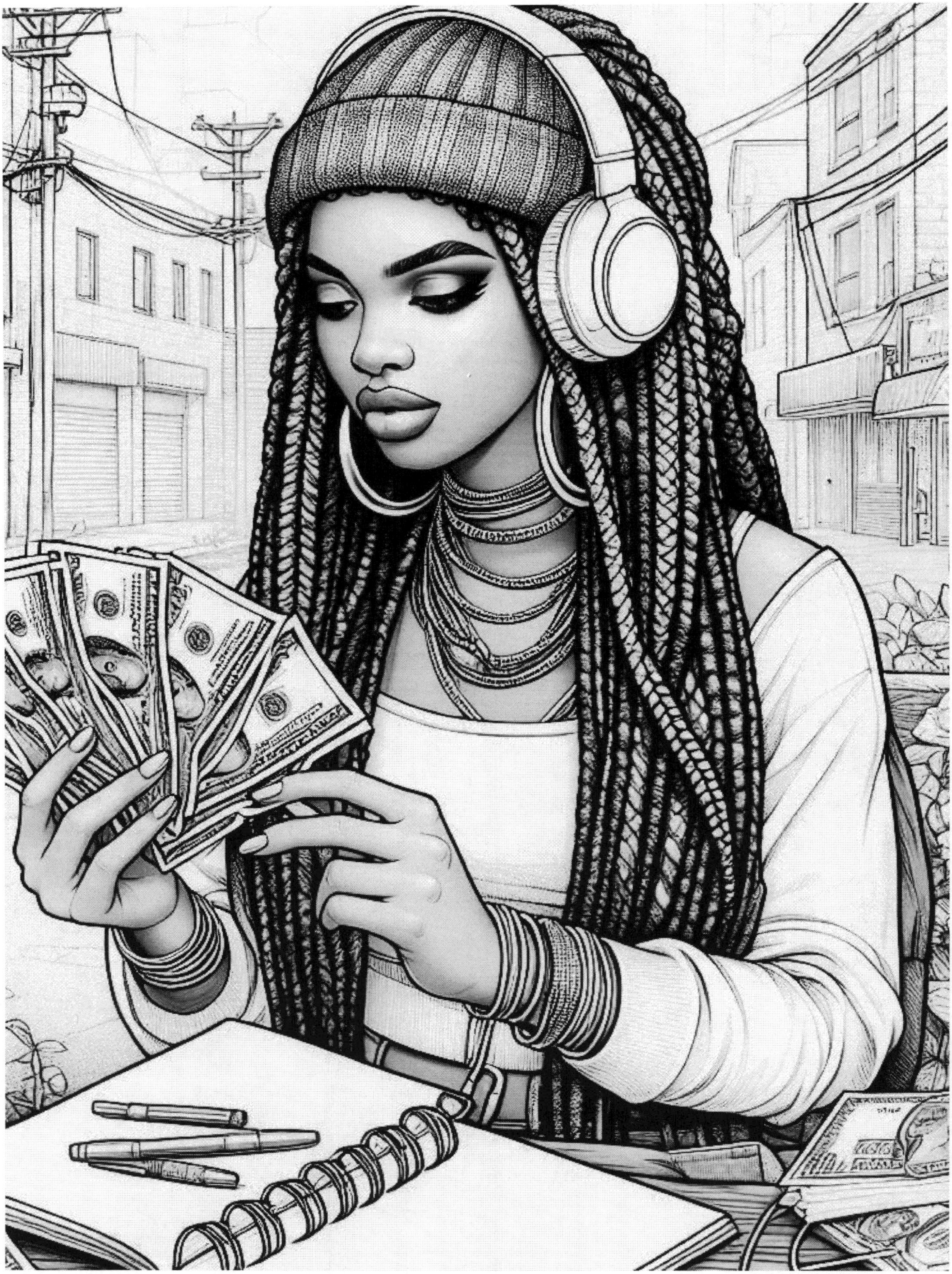

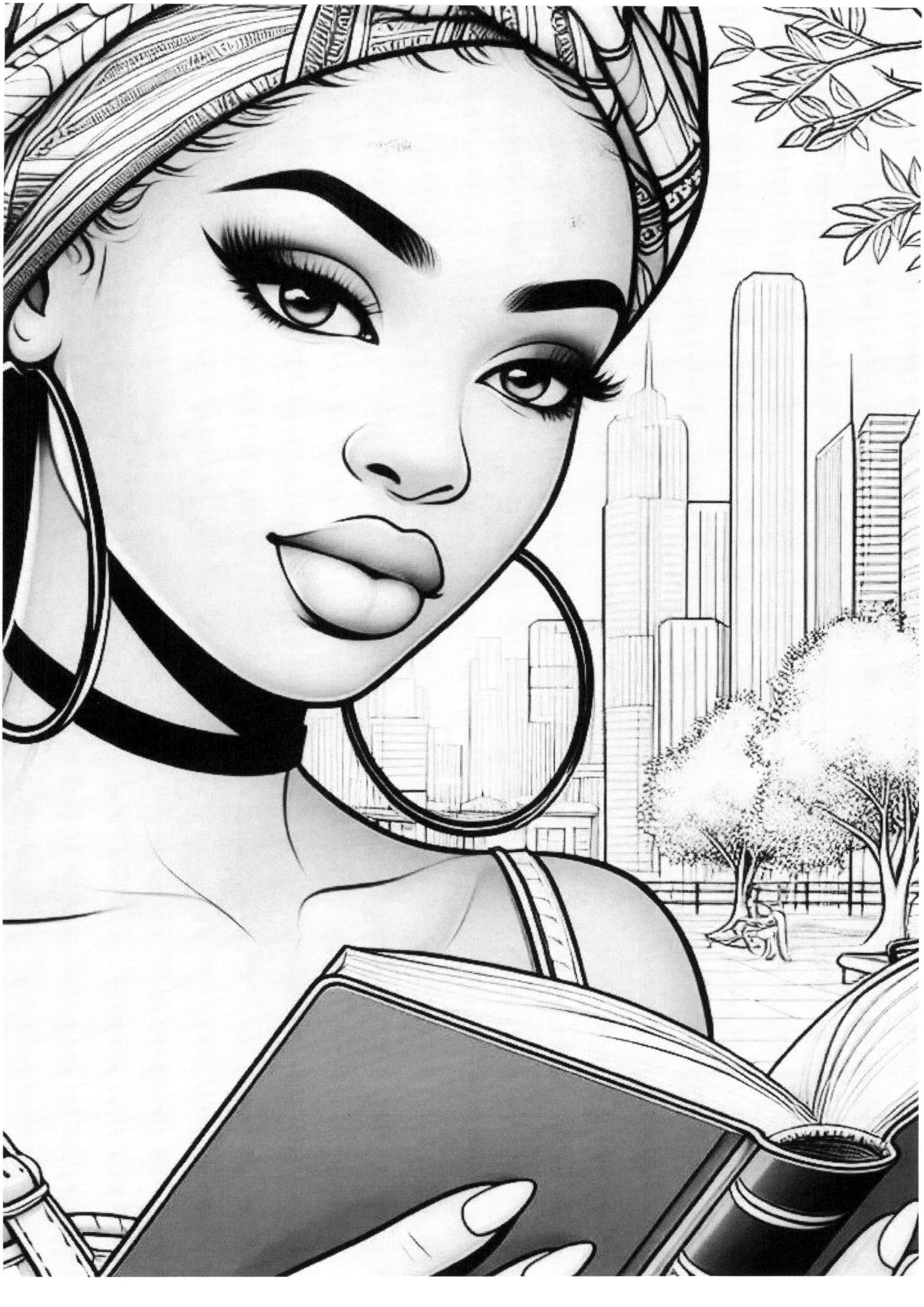

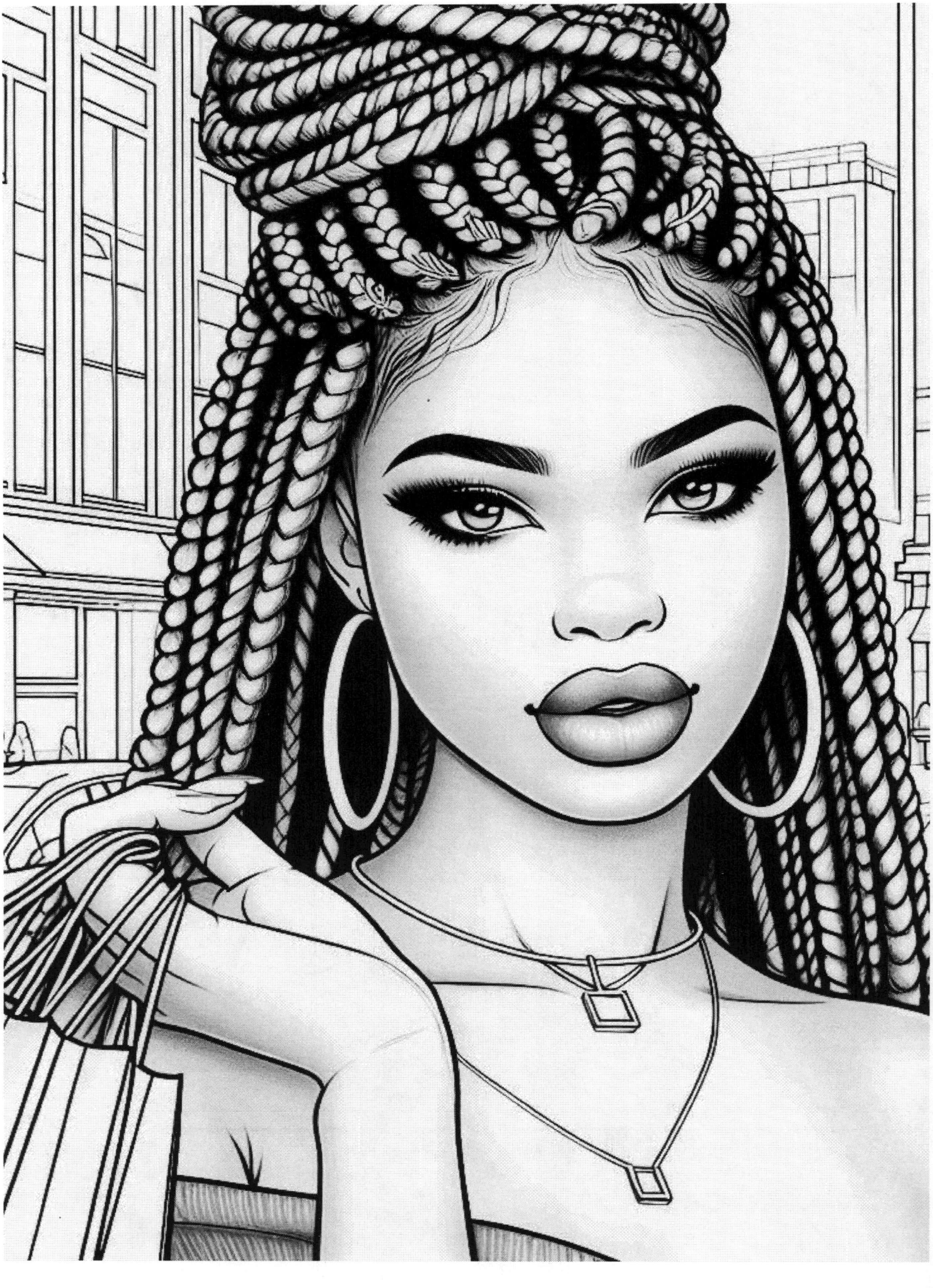

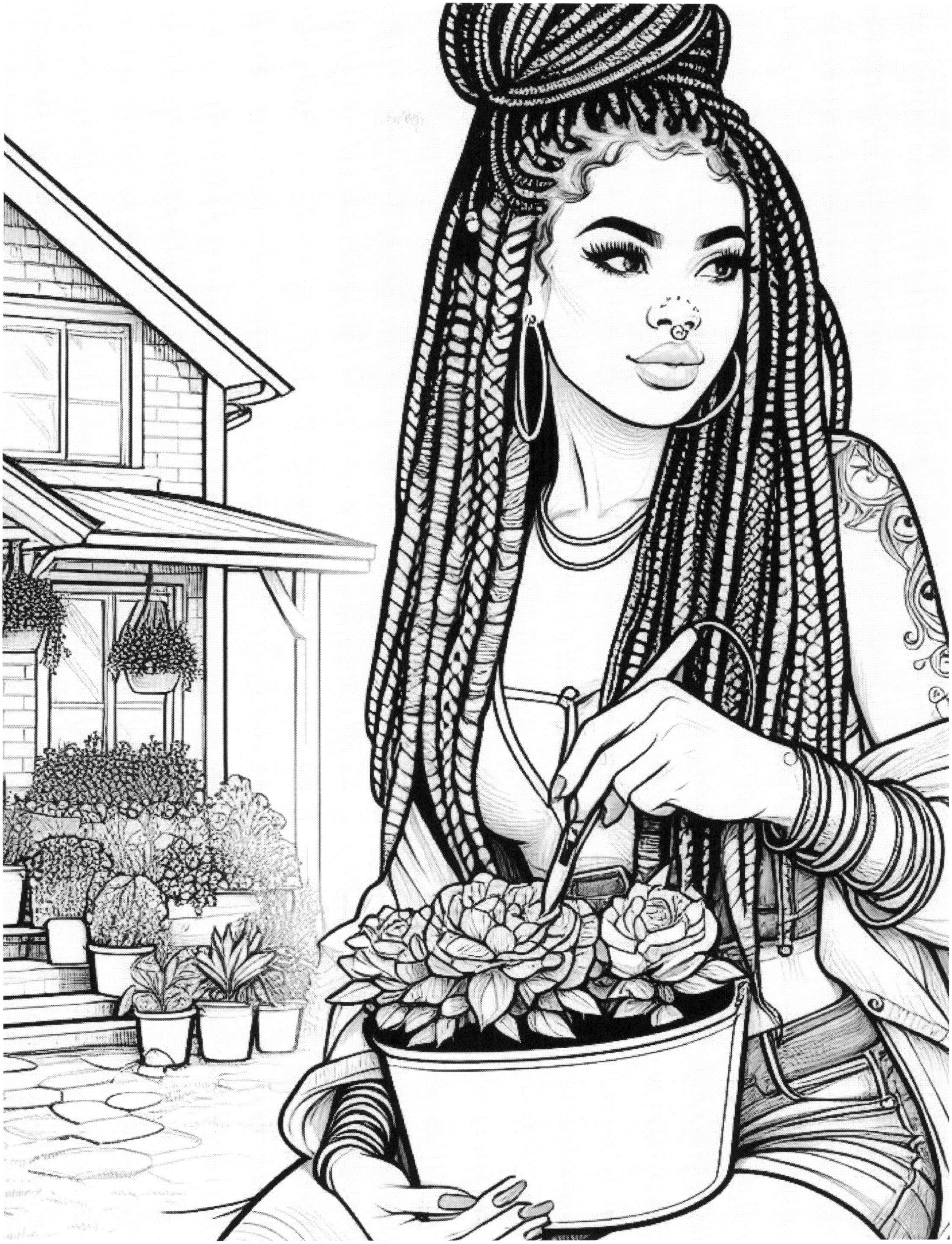

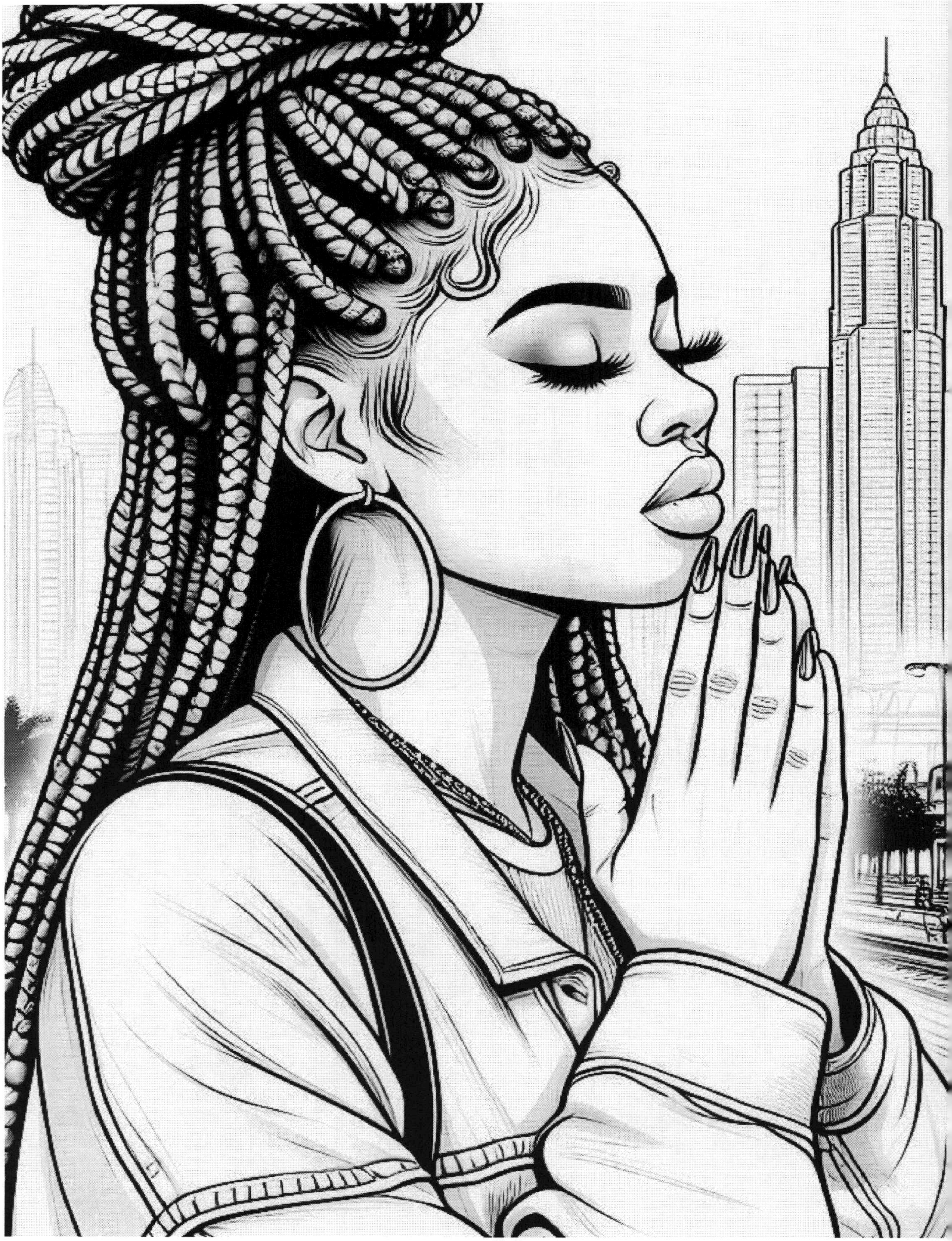

Made in the USA
Middletown, DE
08 March 2024

51081464R00015